My Big Backyard

# Deer

## Lola M. Schaefer

Heinemann Library

Chicago, Illinois

© 2004 Heinemann Library
a division of Reed Elsevier Inc.
Chicago, Illinois

Customer Service  888-454-2279
Visit our website at www.heinemannlibrary.com

Designed by Kim Kovalick, Heinemann Library; Page layout by Que-Net Media
Printed and bound in China by South China Printing Company Limited.
Photo research by Bill Broyles
Edited by Tameika Martin

08 07 06 05 04
10 9 8 7 6 5 4 3 2 1

**Library of Congress Cataloging-in-Publication Data**
Schaefer, Lola M., 1950-
  Deer / Lola M. Schaefer.
      v. cm. – (My big backyard)
Includes bibliographical references (p.      ).
Contents: Are deer in your backyard? – What are deer? – What do deer look like? – How big are deer? – What do deer feel like? – What do deer eat? – What is something special about deer? – How do deer stay safe?
  ISBN 1-4034-5045-5 (hardcover) – ISBN 1-4034-5733-6 (pbk.)
  1.  Deer–Juvenile literature. [1. Deer.]  I. Title.
  QL737.U55S325 2004
  599.65–dc22

                                    2003021018

**Acknowledgments**
The author and publishers are grateful to the following for permission to reproduce copyright material:
pp. 4, 10, 14 Raymond Gehman/Corbis; p. 5 Gary W. Carter/Corbis; p. 6 Darrell Gulin/DRK Photo; pp. 7, 8, 11-13, 15, 16, 19, 21, 22, 24 Stephen J. Krasemann/DRK Photo; p. 9 Jeremy Woodhouse/DRK Photo; p. 17 Corbis; p. 18 Bob Gurr/DRK Photo; p. 20 Kevin R. Morris/Corbis; p. 23 (t-b) Corbis, Corbis, Corbis, Corbis, Stephen J. Krasemann/DRK Photo, Corbis; back cover (l-r) Corbis, Stephen J. Krasemann/DRK Photo

Cover photograph by Tom Brakefield/Corbis

Special thanks to our advisory panel for their help in the preparation of this book:

Eileen Day,
Preschool Teacher
Chicago, IL

Kathleen Gilbert,
Second Grade Teacher
Round Rock, TX

Sandra Gilbert,
Library Media Specialist
Fiest Elementary School
Houston, TX

Jan Gobeille, Kindergarten Teacher
Garfield Elementary
Oakland, CA

Angela Leeper,
Educational Consultant
Wake Forest, NC

Pam McDonald
Reading Teacher
Winter Springs, FL

# Contents

Some words are shown in bold, **like this.**
You can find them in the picture glossary on page 23.

# Are Deer in Your Backyard?

You might see deer in your backyard.

They live all over the world.

Each year there are more deer.

They like to stay in **forests** and thick bushes.

# What Are Deer?

Deer are **mammals.**

Hair covers their bodies.

Deer are warm-blooded.

Their bodies make heat so they can stay warm wherever they are.

# What Do Deer Look Like?

hooves

Deer have long thin bodies.

They have long legs and **hooves**.

Deer have large ears.

They have large eyes, too.

# How Big Are Deer?

Adult deer are as tall as a bicycle.

They weigh as much as
800 hamburgers.

Baby deer are as tall as a
young child.

They weigh as much as
200 hamburgers.

# What Do Deer Feel Like?

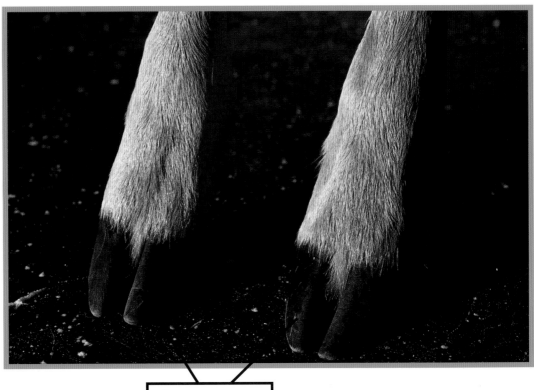

hooves

Deer hair feels very thick.

Their **hooves** are hard like fingernails.

antlers

Deer **antlers** feel smooth with sharp points.

Their tails are soft and fluffy.

# What Do Deer Eat?

Deer might eat grass in your backyard.

They like to eat **acorns,** too.

Deer also eat leaves and fruit.

They eat **grains** from farm fields, too.

# What Is Something Special About Deer?

Male deer grow **antlers**.

Their antlers are made of bone.

Deer have strong legs.

They can run fast and jump high.

# How Do Deer Stay Safe?

Deer stay safe by hiding or running.

They hide in woods and bushes.

Deer are always listening and looking for danger.

When deer get scared, they run away fast.

# Are Deer Dangerous To You?

Deer can be dangerous to people.

Male deer sometime chase people away with their **antlers**.

Does protect their babies.

They may kick with their **hooves.**

# Quiz

What are these deer parts?

**?**

**?**

**?**

**?**

# Picture Glossary

## acorn
page 14
a nut that grows on an oak tree

## antler
pages 13, 16, 20
a horn made of bone that male deer grow on their heads

## forest
page 5
a lot of trees and brushes covering a large area

## grain
page 15
a seed from a plant

## hoof(ves)
pages 8, 12, 21
a hard covering that protects the toes of deer

## mammal
page 6
a warm-blooded animal that is covered in fur or hair

# Note to Parents and Teachers

Reading for information is an important part of a child's literacy development. Learning begins with a question about something. Help children think of themselves as investigators and researchers by encouraging their questions about the world around them. Each chapter in this book begins with a question. Read the question together. Look at the pictures. Talk about what you think the answer might be. Then read the text to find out if your predictions were correct. Think of other questions you could ask about the topic, and discuss where you might find the answers. Assist children in using the picture glossary and the index to practice new vocabulary and research skills.

**!** CAUTION: Remind children that it is not a good idea to handle wild animals. Children should wash their hands with soap and water after they touch any animal.

# Index

**Answers to quiz on page 22**

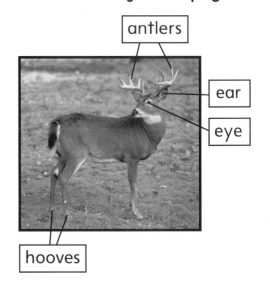

antlers

ear

eye

hooves